Transforming Prayer

Transforming Prayer

10 READY-TO-USE EXPERIENCES

Jenny Baker

First published in 2004 by Spring Harvest Publishing Division and Authentic Media

10 09 08 07 06 05 04   7 6 5 4 3 2 1

Authentic Media, 9 Holdom Avenue, Bletchley, Milton Keynes, Bucks, MK1 1QR, UK
and PO Box 1047, Waynesboro, GA 30830-2047, USA
www.authenticmedia.co.uk

British Library Cataloguing in Publication Data

A catalogue record for this book is available from the British Library

ISBN 1-85078-598-8

Cover design by 4-9-0 ltd
Typeset by Temple Design
Print Management by Adare Carwin

THANK YOU

Thank you to everyone at Grace where most of these ideas developed — Adam, Anna, Harry, Jackie, Joel, Jonny, Mark, Mike, Moya and Steve; thank you to John Buckeridge for your encouragement and opportunities to write.

Contents

Introduction

WHAT HAPPENS WHEN WE PRAY?

Picture the scene. It's the end of the youth group meeting and it's time for the weekly slot of communal prayer. The leader asks if anyone has any needs that they want prayer for and listens to the usual round of requests – help with school work, worry about exams that are coming up, coping with an annoying little brother, sorting out a broken friendship. 'Let's pray,' the leader says and everyone adopts the shampoo position – heads bowed, eyes closed, fingers entwined in their hair. The usual few people pray, and the rest stay silent, a few glancing up now and again to check that the prayer is still going on. The leader wonders what is going on in the minds of the others – are they praying? Or planning their social life for the next week? She finishes with her usual 'And so, Lord, we bring all these prayers to you...' because that's the established signal that the prayer time is over. Heads are lifted; animated conversations start about what's happening during the week; the volume level rises and the youth leader wonders why there is never the same energy and enthusiasm in the prayer time as there is in the rest of the communication that happens among the young people.

Maybe that's a rather gloomy picture of group prayer; maybe it's very different at your church. But that's how many of us learned to pray and that's why so many of us struggle with prayer. I know from my own experience and from talking to young people that very often the desire to pray is there, but it's easy to get distracted and for minds to wander. It can be hard to grasp how prayer works, to see what role we have to play and what difference it can make. And often our attempts at prayer leave us with an overwhelming sense of not being good enough, of not knowing the language or not doing it frequently or fervently enough. When did prayer become something we can fail?

EXPLORING NEW WAYS OF PRAYING

The ideas in this book will explore ways of praying that involve the five senses, using taste, touch, sight, smell and sound to enrich our prayers and help us communicate with God. Many of these prayer ideas involve doing, not just sitting; they enable us to discover truths about prayer as we pray, understanding how it works from what we are engaged in. All the ideas are biblically based, and provide a fresh stimulus to prayer that will spill over into the rest of our lives.

This approach to prayer is not about finding gimmicks to entertain young people or adults while you hope that one day they'll turn up to a 'real' prayer meeting. This is real prayer. This is about encountering God. The activities are not an introduction to prayer – they are the prayer. A youth worker who tried the prayer encounter on page 32, 'A Walk in the Desert' wrote this about the experience:

'I lead a very lively and mixed older girls' youth group. Most of the members are non-Christian from non-Christian families. We decided to try this "experience" with startling results. We didn't use sand but let the girls walk in paint on individual sheets of white paper. Initially it was just a giggle but after about 20 minutes the presence of God could be felt and everyone was writing prayers – either on paper or on their sheet with the footprints. Several girls were in tears. The Pastor of the church was invited and no one wanted the evening to end. Our pastor prayed for each girl in turn and it was a very moving and spiritual evening.'

It's my prayer that the suggestions in this book will enable more people to encounter God in new and surprising ways, discovering how much he loves them and longs to be involved in their world, working with them to extend his kingdom.

ABOUT THIS BOOK

This book contains ten ideas for prayer that can be used as part of a service or group meeting and three self-contained prayer encounters that can be used as a service in their own right. An approximate length of time is included for each idea or encounter as a guide. If you are doing the activity with a large group, it may take a little longer.

DIFFERENT TYPES OF PRAYER

There are lots of different types of prayer and it can be quite difficult to define them. Often we will move from praising God, to asking him for something, to confessing something we have done wrong without even thinking about it. Different types of prayer will overlap and flow into each other and don't need to be too strictly analysed. But for the purpose of this book, these are the definitions I have worked with:

- **Praise** – looking at who God is and giving him praise.
- **Thankfulness** – looking at what God has done for us and thanking him for it.
- **Confession** – telling God about where we have failed him, the sins we have committed, and asking for his forgiveness.
- **Intercession** – specifically praying on behalf of other people – standing in the gap and bringing people that we care for to God.
- **Petition** – asking God to do something for us or for others.
- **Transformation** – prayer that results in ourselves being changed, such as promising God that we will do something, committing ourselves to his service, letting go of the things that trouble us, forgiving others.
- **Prayer of desolation** – a cry of despair from the heart, honest, real prayer that has nowhere else to turn but God.
- **Blessing** – speaking words of God's blessing on people.
- **Contemplation** – the more meditative, silent forms of prayer, listening to God.

The categories of prayer that I have suggested alongside each idea or encounter shouldn't be seen as restrictive; most of them can be adapted to fit other types of prayer.

TEN PRAYER IDEAS

These ideas can be used as part of a worship service, or a group meeting, or on their own. Each idea outlines the supplies that you need, the way you need to set up the idea and what you need to do to lead it. Feel free to adapt these ideas to suit your own talents and creativity, the members of your group and the space that is available to you.

Although each idea is self-explanatory, here are a few things to bear in mind as you plan to run them with your group. The first time you introduce these different methods of praying to your group, you may need to provide lots of reassurance. Explain what will happen during the idea and what people might experience or want to pray about. Once your group have done a few of the ideas you can be less prescriptive, allowing them space to interact with the materials as the Spirit of God leads them.

Pay attention to the surroundings and atmosphere of the environment in which you will pray. Many of the ideas assume people will be sitting on the floor 'in the round' and able to move around freely, rather than in rows of chairs facing the front. You may want to provide cushions for people to sit on. Pay attention to the five senses as you set up the prayer ideas. What will people see, smell, hear, touch and taste during the prayer? There may not be something specifically aimed at each of these senses in all of the prayer ideas – you don't want to overload people after all – but it's worth asking the question. Soft background music played during the prayer can help people relax and not be embarrassed by silence. Low lighting or candles can help people feel less 'on show'.

The ideas can be used with any number of people. If you have a large group, people may need to take it in turns to interact with the materials and it will take longer to do the prayer idea. Be aware of how people are reacting to the prayer experience; it isn't always easy to forgive others or confess sin and these things can't be rushed. Encourage people to talk and pray some more with their friends.

Some of the ideas refer to 'stations', such as prayer idea 4, Standing In The Gap. A station is simply an area that is set up to provide a focus for prayer. Try to make the stations as visually engaging as possible, using images, props and words to stimulate people to pray.

THE PRAYER ENCOUNTERS

These three encounters are self-contained prayer experiences that could be used as a service or group meeting in their own right. All the comments for the prayer ideas above about creating a safe, welcoming prayer environment are relevant, but in addition you may want to consider the following points.

The prayer encounters are written for a facilitator to carry out. You can participate in the prayer if you want to, or remain more detached so that you can observe what is going on and respond accordingly. You can delegate roles or aspects of the encounter to others. It may be helpful to have one or two people who know all about the encounter and can lead the way to show others what to do.

The handouts can be used in different ways. The instructions for the prayer encounter will usually suggest that each person has their own copy of the handout. However, you could put a copy of the words next to a station so that people read it when they get there. Or you could ask someone to read the words at an appropriate point in the experience. These can both help to make the encounter more communal, rather than feeling like isolated individuals going round on their own. You can download full-size copies of the handouts from www.authenticmedia.co.uk.

Tell people how long they have for the prayer encounters. Encourage them to take their time – most activities can be done really quickly but the value is in dwelling with the experience, not racing on to the next bit.

You may need to have someone on hand to look after the materials or stations, to replenish supplies if necessary and make sure that people are using them in the right way.

When clearing up, make sure that any written prayers that have been left behind aren't read by anyone, unless that is a part of the prayer encounter that is understood by everyone before they start writing. You need to respect people's privacy and vulnerability.

A STARTING POINT

This book is intended to be a starting point. It is not a definitive list of methods of prayer by any means. I hope it will spark your imagination once you have experienced for yourself just how transformational prayer ideas like these can be. Involve the members of your group in coming up with creative ideas and planning how to carry them out – I'm sure you'll amaze yourselves at just how innovative and resourceful you can be, and how meaningful the times of prayer are as a result. Above all remember what prayer is all about; communicating with our loving, creator God to know him better and to see his kingdom come on earth as it is in heaven.

What is Prayer?

It feels a little ironic for me to be writing books about prayer. I have kept a journal intermittently over the years and my most frequent entry is 'I must pray more'. I have always struggled with having a regular time for prayer; my prayers are often self-centred or out of desperation; I forget to thank God for answers to prayer. I am not writing this book as a prayer expert (whatever that is), but as someone who still struggles. However, I have also found that thinking a little differently about prayer can have startling results. Finding ways to engage my senses and creativity in prayer has enabled me to actively encounter God in new and surprising ways. Prayer is a fantastic gift from our loving heavenly Father and I'm convinced that many of us never fully unwrap it and discover what it is all about. This book aims to help you do just that, for yourself and for those to whom you minister.

WHAT IS PRAYER?

- Perhaps a good place to start is to remind ourselves just what prayer is.
- Prayer is communication with a Father who loves us, standing alongside our brother Jesus who prays with us.
- Prayer is the discovery of our rightful place, creating in us a wonderful sense of homecoming and belonging.
- Prayer is the relief of bringing the concerns and worries that weigh us down to the God that can deal with them.
- Prayer is the privilege of being involved in God's story of redemption, expecting and waiting for God to change events and change us.
- Prayer is a paradox; it is both a place of safety, where we are most accepted and loved, and a place of risk, of God pushing us out of our comfort zone into new things.
- Prayer is the loneliest, most desolate place at times, where the deepest and most distressing cries of the human heart are heard.
- Prayer is a creative adventure; there are no formulas or guarantees of 'success'.

SO WHY IS PRAYER OFTEN SO DIFFICULT?

I think there are three main reasons why we often struggle with prayer.

We are creative communicators but often our prayer follows a formula.

Think for a moment of someone you love – your mum or dad, your girlfriend or husband. How would you communicate your love to that person without words? You might buy them a gift, write them a note, cook their favourite meal, clean their car for them, run them a scented, candle-lit bath – I'm sure you can think of lots more ways. We are creative people who communicate with each other in many different ways and yet when we pray we follow the 'hands together, eyes closed' formula.

Like Pavlov's dog, we have a conditioned response to the phrase 'Let's pray'! We tend to shut down all the creativity that we use so effortlessly in the rest of our lives. There is something beautiful about stillness, about centring on God and being quiet, and some of these prayer ideas explore that aspect further. But why in prayer do we shut down and restrict our means of expression instead of using our God-given creativity and talent?

Reducing prayer to a formula sends out the message that prayer has a code of conduct, that you mustn't get it wrong. Instead of focusing on our relationship with God, we are focusing on what we are doing and whether we are getting it right. Are we using the right language? Have we gone on for long enough? Are we just repeating what someone else said? Have we missed anything out?

The other message that we pick up from the 'hands together, eyes closed' formula is that when we pray, we shut out the rest of the world. There is some wisdom in that; it's good to stop distractions and focus on God. But we also need to be able to bring the reality of our world to God in prayer. Instead of prayer being a place where we become super-spiritual in order to impress God, prayer should be a place where we bring our frail and vulnerable selves in order to become more like Jesus.

The culture around us engages us with complex and interactive communication but often our prayer feels like we are talking to the ceiling.

Young people today are surrounded by slick commercials, sophisticated images, and interactive ways to communicate with each other and the world around them, and it's all intuitive to them. Emails, text messages, phone polls on TV and radio, mobile phones and the Internet all provide the means to get their voice heard and have an impact on their surroundings. In contrast, prayer can seem like an alien language that needs to be learned. The old saying 'I hear and I forget; I see and I remember; I do and I understand' encapsulates the way they explore the world around them, experientially, actively, instantly. Of course, any form of prayer can give us an experience of God, but providing prayer activities that engage the senses and involve doing as well as being somehow connect with this generation that was born with a computer mouse in their hand. And it's not just young people who will benefit. These prayer ideas can be used with people of all ages and at all stages of their Christian life.

We are all different, unique individuals, but often we only make available one model of prayer.

If I have spent all day working at my computer, I may choose to go for a run to relax and unwind. I want some space to myself and to do something physical rather than use my brain. Someone else might get on the phone after a hard day at work and spend all evening discussing the events of the day with her friends. Another person might want to 'veg' in front of the TV, not moving or speaking, just being entertained; someone else will go out and socialize, making the most of his free time. These different activities might all have the same result – helping us to relax and leave behind the stresses of the day – but each is suited to the personality of the person who chose it.

Different people are energised and drained by different things, communicating with those around them in different ways. Always following the same model of prayer will leave a lot of us frustrated and silenced, unable to make the most of it and feeling we just can't do it. Just having one means of expressing prayer limits our understanding of God and the ways in which he might communicate with us.

Prayer does not need to be a 'one-size-fits-all' experience. Prayer can be creative, interactive and engaging.

These prayer ideas and encounters will help overcome some of these difficulties and enable people to communicate with God in a new way. Transforming our understanding of what a time of prayer could look, sound, smell, taste and feel like will lead to encounters with God in prayer that will in turn transform us and our world. Try it and see!

Prayer ideas

PRAYER IDEA

Standing In The Gap

Scripture Focus:	1 Samuel 7:2-6
Type of Prayer:	intercession
Time Needed:	45 minutes
Supplies:	cross – either one that is used in your church worship, or one that you make out of pieces of wood. It needs to be quite large to provide a good focal point at the center of the room; 4 large pieces of card; materials to inform prayers – such as newspaper headlines, pictures, names of people who are in need; pens

OVERVIEW

Intercession is praying to God for other people, standing in the gap between them and God and bringing their needs before him. This activity illustrates this by getting people to join hands as they pray, forming a human connection between the cross and the need for prayer. By acting out the spiritual reality and physically bridging the gap between God and the need, it reminds people of what they are doing and helps them grasp the significance of their prayers.

SETUP

You will need an empty room. Set up the cross in the middle of the room. Decide on four things that you want to encourage people to pray about – perhaps people who are ill or in need, people who don't know Christ, situations of conflict around the world and situations of need in the neighborhood. Set up a station for each of these, one on each of the four walls of the room. Each station should be a piece of card stuck on the wall with a title telling people what to pray about, and some inspiration for prayer stuck around it such as pictures, words, newspaper headlines and so on. Put some pens under the board so that people can write up their own ideas for prayer. Experiment to see how many people are needed to link hands and form a human chain between the cross and each station; this will tell you how many people need to be in each small group.

THE IDEA

Ask people to sit on the floor around the cross. Explain what the word intercession means – standing in the gap between God and someone in need and bringing that need to God in prayer. Explain that this activity will enable people to spend some time in intercession, praying for people and situations in need.

Invite people to go round the room, visiting each of the four stations in turn, identifying needs for prayer at each and writing them up on the card. Allow about fifteen minutes for them to do this.

Now comes the actual prayer. Illustrate how this will work with a few people. Hold hands in a chain so that one person touches the cross and the person at the other end touches the wall. The person next to the cross prays first for the need on their heart and then each person in turn prays. If people are not used to praying out loud in front of others, they can pray silently and then say 'Amen' aloud to indicate when they have finished. Allow plenty of time for people to move around the room and pray. After 20 to 25 minutes, or earlier if people are running out of steam, tell people that they have one more minute in which to finish their prayers. After that minute call everyone together and lead them in thanking God that he had heard their prayers and will answer in his way and in his time.

Extra

As an alternative for a small group, attach lengths of ribbon to the cross and to the bottom of each piece of card. The ribbons need to be long enough so that when they are connected they lie on the floor between the wall and the cross – otherwise your prayer time will be more like an assault course! Start the activity in the same way, but when it comes to praying, ask people to go round in twos. At each station, one person collects the end of a ribbon attached to the cross and the other collects the end attached to the station. As they pray for the need, they tie the two ribbons together, bridging the gap between the two and leaving a physical reminder of their prayer.

Round The Clock

Scripture Focus:	1 Thessalonians 5:16-18
Type of Prayer:	thankfulness
Time Needed:	one hour
Supplies:	15 large sheets of paper, drawing pins or blu-tack, a rubber stamp for each participant, 15 ink pads, colored pens

OVERVIEW

When did you last thank God for the bed that you sleep in, or the clothes that you put on, or the Bible that you read? There is so much we could thank God for, and yet so often we just take it all for granted. This activity will help your group heed Paul's advice and 'give thanks in all circumstances', by prompting them to find a way to say thank you for almost anything. When we start thanking God for even very basic everyday things, we begin to appreciate how truly blessed we are and praise and thankfulness just flows!

SETUP

Write an hour of the day on each of the large sheets of paper, from 8am to 10pm. Stick these up around the room and put pens and a colored inkpad near each one. Have the rubber stamp for each person ready to hand out for the second half of the activity; if you have a large group you may want to give them each a colored pen and ask them to sign their initials instead of using a rubber stamp. Choose which day in the last week will be the focus of your thankfulness.

THE IDEA

This activity is in two stages. First, ask everyone to go round the room and write up on each sheet of paper what they were doing at that time on the specific day that you have chosen. They will all need to start at different places, and it doesn't matter if they write similar things to each other. This will take about twenty minutes and will give you a wonderful record of a day in the life of your youth group!

During the second half of the activity, people will revisit each of the sheets, choose something that is written up there, and they will find something to thank God for in their own experience, praying until they are truly thankful. So for example, if someone had written up 'maths lesson', they may not have had a maths lesson themselves that week and may not genuinely be grateful for maths, but they could thank God for the education that they have had when so many children and young people around the world can't even go to school. Once they have done that, they stamp that activity with their rubber stamp or sign their initials. At the next sheet they choose something that hasn't yet been stamped and thank God for it.

Before they set off, demonstrate how this will work for the group by talking through what a couple of the different activities might prompt you to thank God for. So for example, for any comments related to school, you could thank God for good teachers that you have learned from or the support your parents have given you in your education. If someone had written up 'went home', you could thank God for your own home and all he has provided for you. Even if someone has written up something horrible that has happened to them, like 'had an argument with my friend', you could thank God for your own friends, for their loyalty even through difficult times, and you could add a prayer that the person who had had the argument would be able to resolve it. Providing concrete examples like this will help young people grasp what they need to do.

Hand out the rubber stamps and tell them to start giving thanks. Allow lots of time for people to go round and give thanks. If people get stuck, encourage them to talk to each other about what they could give thanks for. You could play some praise or worship music in the background during this prayer time to provide a good backdrop to the prayers.

TRANSFORMING PRAYER

6

After half an hour or so of people praying and stamping the comments, call everyone together. Get them to chant together three times 'For all you have given us, Lord we thank you' to end the prayer time.

PRAYER IDEA

River Of Justice

Scripture Focus: Amos 5:24

Type of Prayer: petition, intercession, praise

Time Needed: 30 minutes

Supplies: long streamers of blue paper, three or four for each participant – different shades of blue look very effective; information about situations of injustice such as countries where there is poverty, or where Christians are persecuted, or people are suffering from HIV/AIDS, or situations of conflict; small pieces of card and pens

OVERVIEW

It's difficult to pray for big issues like poverty or famine or HIV/AIDS. The problems seem so complex and hard to solve that it can be difficult to see how our prayers can make any difference at all. But if the complexity and injustice of these situations stops us praying, then we are ignoring one of our key weapons in the fight for a fairer world. Amos uses the image of a river to talk about God's justice, sweeping over everything in its path, not stopping for anyone, powerful and majestic.

SETUP

Think about how you will inform your group about a situation of injustice in the world – a country where there is poverty, or where Christians are persecuted, or people are suffering from HIV/AIDS, or situations of conflict. You could do this through pictures, stories, video or inviting someone to talk to the group. Choose the area where you will lay out the river of justice – the aisle of the church would be a good place. The streamers of blue paper will need to be as long as this area. Put them at one end with the cards and pens.

THE IDEA

Spend some time with your group learning about the situation of injustice. You could give the group some different magazine articles to read in pairs and then ask them to report back to the others a one-minute summary of what they have learned. Talk about why this injustice has arisen and what the group can do about it. Remind them of God's heart for justice and his power to change people and situations. Invite people to put items that represent the injustice along the area you have chosen for the river to be laid out. These could be pictures, some words they have written on cards or anything else they can think of. This part should take 10 to 15 minutes.

Then hand out the long streamers of blue paper. Ask people to walk down the aisle of the church praying for the situation of injustice. As they pray they should lay out their streamer around and over the symbols of injustice. Each person could return to pray several times, laying down another streamer. Each time they return to pray for the situation, they will see more evidence of other people's prayers that will boost their faith. Remind them that some prayers could focus on who God is, praising him for his ability to intervene. Once all the streamers have been used, gather around the river and finish the prayer time by praying these words of Amos together: 'Let justice roll on like a river and righteousness like a never-failing stream.'

PRAYER IDEA

Monument

Scripture Focus: Joshua 4:1-9

Type of Prayer: praise, thankfulness

Time Needed: 30 minutes

Supplies: colored chalks, large stones – one for every three or four participants

OVERVIEW

Throughout the Old Testament, God tells the Israelites to remember their history. Telling the stories of where they have come from and of God's dealings with them gives them direction and hope for the future. This remembering happened through rituals, feasts and memorials like the one in this story from the book of Joshua. Joshua set up twelve stones to remind the people of Israel that the waters of the Jordan had parted to allow them to cross – one stone for each of the tribes of Israel. This activity works well at the end of a camp or mission trip, or after an event or project that people have worked on together. Or you can use it to look back on the last six months or year in the life of your group.

SETUP

Choose a suitable site for the monument – a park or field, or a corner of a garden or car park. Think about how many stones it is appropriate to have in the monument. You could ask people to get into groups of three or four to talk about what they want to commemorate. Or you could have one stone for each tent in a camp or each group involved in a project. Check that there are enough large stones around. If not, you will need to get some from a garden center, a beach or your own garden.

THE IDEA

Ask a volunteer to read aloud the story of this monument from Joshua 4:1-9. Ask people to get into groups of three or four, or into the groups that they were in at camp or on the project. Each group needs to find a large stone and talk about what God has done for them during the trip or project, or they could look back over the last six months and reflect on how God has been active in their lives. They can then chalk words or symbols on their stone to symbolize these things as they pray, thanking God for what he has done. Allow 15 minutes for people to discuss in groups and decorate their stone.

Then gather everyone around the site where you are going to build the monument. Ask the groups to step forward one by one, place their stone on the monument, and spend a couple of minutes sharing with everyone else what they want to commemorate by placing their stone. Make sure the stones are firmly set on top of each other; you will probably need to put larger stones at the base and taper the monument towards the top. Take time to build something sturdy. Ask someone to pray aloud on behalf of the whole group.

Extra

Remind the group that the Israelites were told to be ready to answer the question, 'What do these stones mean?' How will they answer when their friends and family ask what these stones are here for? You could bring the group back to the monument on the anniversary of its making, to remember what God has done in the past, and to reflect on whether God is still as active in their lives today. The chalk marks will fade in the rain, but hopefully the memories they have will remain.

Autumn

Scripture Focus:	Psalm 88; Genesis 8:22
Type of Prayer:	prayer of desolation
Time Needed:	15 minutes
Supplies:	dried leaves – one for each participant plus a few extra for visual effect

OVERVIEW

A whole range of emotions is expressed in the Psalms – joy, delight, excitement, anger, envy, vengeance, sorrow, pain and, as in Psalm 88, desolation and despair. Many of the darker psalms end with a note of hope, the decision of the psalmist to praise God in spite of his situation and feelings, but even that is missing in this psalm.

In our churches we can often feel that we need to always be on top of things – happy, full of faith, triumphant and trusting. And yet as Christians we are not immune to sorrow and pain. Instead of feeling under pressure to pretend that everything is OK, we need to have space to bring our real emotions to God like the psalmists did. This prayer idea will enable people to express their brokenness and pain, and will remind them that God is able to heal and restore them.

SETUP

Collect some dried leaves that have fallen from trees and arrange them in a central place for people to come and collect one. If you are doing this in a different season from the autumn and there are no dried leaves around, look for other things in nature that seem dead or dried up – pine cones, dead branches, dried flowers or grasses.

THE IDEA

Ask a volunteer to read aloud Psalm 88. Remind people that they can be honest before God about their feelings, even if they are feeling far from him.

Invite people to take a dried leaf and hold it as they pray to God about the things in their lives that seem dead and dried up. Allow ten minutes or so for people to think and pray.

God promises that seasons will always follow one another. Read Genesis 8:22 and say the following as the participants hold the dead leaves.

'As long as the earth endures,
seedtime and harvest,
cold and heat,
summer and winter,
day and night will never cease.'

Imagine what a tree looks like as it goes through the seasons of the year. In the autumn, the leaves change color and fall from the tree. In winter the tree is bare and there is little sign of life. After months of cold, in spring small streaks of green appear as buds open and new leaves unfurl. In summer the tree's branches are heavy with leaves; a wonderful green canopy shades the ground from the sun. And then a few weeks later, the cycle begins again.

Just as spring follows winter, so God will bring new life out of pain and brokenness. That does not negate or deny what we are feeling, but encourages us to look forward to what God will do. Let's give these leaves and our feelings back to God and ask him to transform them.

Walk among the participants and gather up their leaves. Stand in front of everyone holding the leaves and lead them in offering to God the feelings and situations they represent, asking him to bring new life in the middle of pain.

Extra

Just as some people will find it hard to sing happy songs when they are feeling desolate, so some people will find it hard to identify with this activity when they are feeling joyful and close to God. You could encourage those for whom this activity is not directly relevant to pray for someone that they know who is going through a difficult time.

PRAYER IDEA

Newspaper Prayers

Scripture Focus:	Isaiah 58:1-9; Ephesians 3:20,21
Type of Prayer:	intercession, petition
Time Needed:	30 minutes
Supplies:	newspapers, bold colored paints, brushes, a large notice board to make a collage, glue

OVERVIEW

Praying for national or international situations can feel like building a barrier with sand to stop the tide coming in. However hard you work, your efforts feel futile and unable to make any difference. But we mustn't forget who we are praying to. Although we as individuals may not be able to change much, we pray to a God who is able to transform situations by his power. And our efforts combined with those of our brothers and sisters can have an impact beyond our expectations.

SETUP

Collect together the supplies and set them out in front of the notice board on the wall. The newspapers need to be in black and white to get the best impact. You may want to cover the floor to protect it from paint. If you have a large group, you may need more than one notice board. Plan on having one notice board for every twenty people doing the prayer activity.

THE IDEA

Invite people to cut out situations that need prayer from the newspapers and stick them onto the notice board in a collage; these can be from countries overseas as well as needs closer to home. You could get people to work in twos or threes, so they can talk about why they are choosing those particular situations. Get them to cut out the whole article – including the headline, text and any picture, so there is lots for them to paint over later. The collage should fill the whole notice board. The newspaper stories can overlap each other and it doesn't matter if it looks rather disorganized and chaotic. The collage will take about ten minutes to create.

Once everyone has added their newspaper cuttings to the collage and it is finished, ask people to pray for these situations and, as they do so, to paint over the situation they are praying for with a color – not obliterating it, but painting over grace and justice, praying that God will bring about transformation. You may need to ask people to take it in turns to paint; allow four or five people at a time at the notice board for three minutes, then allow other people to have a turn. Those who are not painting can still be praying, on their own or in twos or threes. If someone gets to the notice board and finds their chosen subject has already been prayed for, they can pray for it nonetheless and add some more paint, or they can choose a new situation to pray for. Keep swapping round until all the situations are prayed for.

Ask someone to read Ephesians 3:20,21 aloud during the painting to inspire people to be bold in prayer. God is able to do immeasurably more than all we can ask or imagine.

Invite everyone to stand back and appreciate the revolution that has taken place – color has replaced the black and white. The collage could be left up in the church or room for a few weeks to remind people what they have prayed for, and to look for answers to prayer.

PRAYER IDEA

The Aroma Of Christ

Scripture Focus:	2 Corinthians 2:14-16
Type of Prayer:	intercession, petition
Time Needed:	15 minutes
Supplies:	perfume, cologne or scented oil – have two or three different scents available; card, pens, paint, paintbrushes

OVERVIEW

Smells can have a powerful effect on us. The smell of bacon frying can make your mouth water and create a fantastic sense of expectation of the breakfast that is to come. The scent of a stranger's perfume in a crowd can remind you of someone you love and make you smile as you think of them. Paul uses this wonderful image of us spreading the fragrance of the knowledge of Christ wherever we go, causing people to sit up and notice and want to know more.

SETUP

Choose perfumes or scented oils that will appeal to both males and females in your group. Set out the card, pens, paint and paintbrushes so that everyone will have easy access to them.

THE IDEA

Invite people to think of a friend or family member that does not know Christ and pray for opportunities to speak to them, or demonstrate the love of Christ to them. As they pray they should write the person's name on a card, decorating it with pictures/symbols that remind them of that person – what they do, where they live, the members of their family. They should

17

pray about each thing as they draw. Tell them that they will have about fifteen minutes to decorate the card.

When the card is finished, each person should spray perfume on themselves and the card, or use the scented oil, to remind themselves that they will be the aroma of Christ to the person they have prayed for.

They can take the card with them to remind them to keep praying, or give it to the person for whom they have prayed.

PRAYER IDEA

Internet Prayers

Scripture Focus:	Romans 1:8-10
Type of Prayer:	intercession, petition, blessing
Time Needed:	30 minutes
Supplies:	computers with Internet access – you'll need one computer for every four or five people

OVERVIEW

The Internet has enabled people to communicate with each other across the world like never before. It can also help us to pray for each other. www.rejesus.co.uk is one site where you can pray and light a virtual candle that will 'burn' for the next 36 hours. You can also read the prayers that other people around the world have prayed, and get a sense of the worldwide nature of the body of Christ.

SETUP

Visit www.rejesus.co.uk to familiarize yourself with the prayer board. From the home page, click on the Spirituality section, click on Post a prayer and then click to launch the Post a prayer section (or if you don't mind typing in a long url, go straight to www.rejesus.co.uk/spirituality/post_prayer/index.html). Read some of the prayers that are already there and follow the instructions to add your own prayers. If you are using this prayer idea with a small group of less than ten, use a computer in someone's home and take it in turns to pray and add a candle. If you are leading a larger group, visit an Internet café together and use different terminals to access the prayer board, or one of the other sites mentioned below. See if you can book a session on several computers at the Internet café for the time when you need it, or choose a time when it's not too busy.

THE IDEA

Gather participants together somewhere you can talk together. Introduce the idea of praying with Christians from all over the world. Find out who has Christian friends and family in different countries. Then go to the computers and access the Internet. Visit the Post a prayer section of the www.rejesus.co.uk website. If you are in an Internet café using several computers, write out the website address and instructions from the Setup section on pieces of card, so that each small group knows what to do. If this site is not available, suggest that they do an Internet search using the words 'prayer forum' or 'prayer board' to find another suitable site.

Once the site has been accessed, get people to read some of the prayers that have been posted recently; each person in the group could add their own silent prayer for that situation as they read them. Then allow people to take it in turns to pray and add their own prayers to the board. They could send an email to the person they have prayed for, telling them about the prayer and the website.

Extra

Another site to visit is www.24-7prayer.com, the home of the 24-7 prayer movement. The Wailing Wall section of the site has lots of prayers from people all over the world and enables you to add your own.

Extra

You could set up a website for your own group where they can post their prayers or prayer requests. One of your group members may know how to do it, if your technological expertise doesn't extend that far! Or you could set up an email list, where a prayer request or daily prayer can be sent round all the members of the group that are on email.

PRAYER IDEA

Tree Of Life

Scripture Focus: Revelation 22:1-5

Type of Prayer: intercession, petition

Time Needed: 30 minutes

Supplies: large branch – it will look good if it is as tall as an adult; tree stand or large pot and stones; streamers of green paper; pens

OVERVIEW

We live in anticipation of Christ's return, knowing that he has defeated sin and death on the cross but still living in a broken and fallen world. We look forward to the time when there will be no more sickness, pain or tears and we can pray for God's healing now as a foretaste of that new reality. This prayer idea uses an image from Revelation to help us pray for healing for people that we know and the world that we live in.

SETUP

Get hold of a fairly large branch of a tree – the more small twigs at the end the better, so that it looks like a miniature tree. Fix it so that it stands upright. You could use a Christmas tree stand – the kind that has clamps that you can tighten against a tree trunk – or put the bottom of the branch into a large pot and add some bricks and stones to hold it upright. It would be a good idea to have someone to hold the tree upright for safety while people are attaching their prayers.

You can buy streamers of paper or cut them from large sheets. Have the streamers of paper and pens accessible to everyone.

THE IDEA

Ask a volunteer to read Revelation 22:1-5 aloud to set the context for the time of prayer. Invite people to think of a person or a situation that they know needs healing. They can collect a streamer of paper and a pen and write out their prayer for that person on the paper. After about five minutes, when they have finished, invite them to come up a few at a time and carefully tie their prayer onto the branch so that it looks like a leaf of the tree. The streamers can hang down like leaves in a willow tree, or be gently tied into bows to look like several leaves on a branch.

Each person can write more than one prayer, returning to the tree to add another leaf. When everyone has finished praying, ask them to stand and look at the tree – instead of a bare branch there are now leaves, a symbol of the new life and hope that Jesus can bring to those in need.

Extra

An alternative way of using this same Bible passage is to draw a large, bare tree on a sheet of paper. Use paints to color in the bark. Give people leaf shapes cut out of green paper on which to write their prayers and get them to stick these to the end of the branches to create a leafy tree.

Nails

Scripture Focus:	Isaiah 53:4-6; Colossians 2:13-15
Type of Prayer:	confession
Time Needed:	15 minutes
Supplies:	nails, hammers, large piece of wood, scented oil

OVERVIEW

God's grace and forgiveness are freely given, but they are not cheap. Our redemption was paid for by Jesus on the cross. We can come to God at any time and as often as we like to confess our sin and ask for forgiveness, and we will receive it. But sometimes it is good to dwell on what it cost Jesus to set us free from sin. This prayer idea does that, not to make us feel even more guilty, but to increase our thankfulness and praise for what Jesus has done.

SETUP

Simply set out the piece of wood with the hammer and nails next to it. Have the bottle of scented oil nearby so that people can use it to anoint themselves.

THE IDEA

Encourage people to make themselves comfortable and relax. Give them an opportunity to think about the last week and the things they have done wrong. You could use these words that follow, or some words of your own. You may not want to focus on just the last week, but enable people to think about things further back in the past. Leave pauses to enable people to reflect and pray.

Think back over the last week and all that you have done.

Invite the Holy Spirit to walk with you back through the last few days and show you where you have sinned, where your thoughts and actions have created distance between you and God.

Perhaps in the things that you have done that have harmed others;

Or in failing to take action where you could have spread God's love.

Perhaps in the things you have said,

Or the things that you left unsaid.

Perhaps in your thoughts.

Confess these things to God, and ask for his forgiveness.

Read Isaiah 53:4-6.

'Surely he took up our infirmities and carried our sorrows, yet we considered him stricken by God, smitten by him, and afflicted.

But he was pierced for our transgressions, he was crushed for our iniquities; the punishment that brought us peace was upon him, and by his wounds we are healed.

We all, like sheep, have gone astray, each of us has turned to his own way; and the Lord has laid on him the iniquity of us all.'

Invite people to come and hammer a nail into the piece of wood, in recognition that it was their sin that caused Jesus to go to the cross. Allow about ten minutes for this part.

They can then make the sign of the cross on their forehead in scented oil as a symbol that they are forgiven. The smell of the oil throughout the remainder of the day will remind them of what Jesus has done for them. People could put oil on one another's foreheads and speak God's forgiveness to each other or you could have one person who makes a cross in oil on everyone's forehead and speaks God's anointing and forgiveness over them.

When everyone has had the opportunity to do this, read Colossians 2:13-15.

'When you were dead in your sins and in the uncircumcision of your sinful nature, God made you alive with Christ. He forgave us all our sins, having cancelled the written code with its regulations, that was against us and that stood opposed to us; he took it away, nailing it to the cross. And having disarmed the powers and authorities, he made a public spectacle of them, triumphing over them by the cross.'

Lead a prayer of thanks and praise for what Jesus has done on the cross. Encourage others to pray prayers of thanks and worship, or sing some worship songs together. End the prayer time on a note of worship and adoration rather than the solemnity of the nails in wood.

Prayer Encounters

Bread

Scripture Focus: Psalm 13

Type of Prayer: transformation, contemplation

Time Needed: 30 minutes

Supplies: Some bread dough – you can use a 'just-add-water' mix or start from scratch with yeast and flour. An electronic bread-maker is useful – if you haven't got one ask around to see if you can borrow one.

Some bread for each person to eat. You could buy some bread or have baking trays and extra dough to bake bread rolls, if there is an oven at the venue.

A copy of the handout for each participant. You can download full-size copies of the handouts from www.authenticmedia.co.uk.

Bibles – have one for every two or three participants.

OVERVIEW

Our prayers are seldom answered in exactly the way we expect. God often surprises us by doing something new and different, and answering our prayer in far better ways than we could ever have imagined. But sometimes it seems like nothing is happening – our prayers go unanswered. While we know in our heads that God's ways and his timing are perfect, we can feel let down when it seems like there is no response. Has God heard? Did we use the wrong words? Perhaps there's something between God and us?

These are all good questions to ask, but we don't often get the space to ask them.

This prayer encounter will allow people to voice their feelings about unanswered prayer and to reflect on the fact that God answers prayers in his way and time, not ours.

Using the handout as a guide, people will think about the way that bread is made. It's a slow process of providing the right conditions and waiting for the yeast to do its work. Homemade bread can't be rushed, but the taste at the end is worth all the waiting. People will be invited to take some of the dough and knead it in their hands as they tell God about the answers to prayer that they are still waiting for. They will read David's cry from the heart in Psalm 13, where he feels abandoned by God but still chooses to trust him. Then they will have the opportunity to eat some bread to show that they choose to trust God to satisfy their hunger.

SETUP

You'll need a space where people can sit round the bowl of dough in the center. Use background music, candles, and cushions to create a comfortable atmosphere. If you've got access to an oven, make extra dough and shape some of it into bread rolls. Put these on baking trays and set one beside the bowl of dough at the start. Switch the oven on in advance so it is nice and hot; bread usually cooks at around 200° to 220°C (400° to 450°F) but check the bread-dough packet or recipe you are using to get the right temperature. If you don't have an oven, buy some nice bread to give out at the end of the prayer encounter. Make sure the Bibles are accessible to everyone.

THE ENCOUNTER

Ask people to sit around the bowl of dough and make themselves comfortable. Introduce the theme and ask people to think about where they are waiting for answers to prayer. What have they prayed for? How long have they been waiting? How do they feel about it? Encourage them to be honest.

Give out copies of the handout and allow people space to read, reflect and pray. You could put the bread rolls in the oven at this stage – they usually take about 15 minutes to cook but follow the directions on the packet or in the recipe.

You will be able to see when individuals have read Psalm 13. After they have had time to pray about it, take some bread round to each person, or invite them to give bread to each other. Use words of encouragement such as 'God will satisfy your hunger for him' or Matthew 5:6: 'Blessed are those who hunger and thirst for righteousness for they shall be filled.'

After about 25 minutes, end with a time of prayer all together, thanking God for his love and provision, acknowledging that he knows what is best for us and will answer the cries of our heart in his way and time, and asking for God's help to be patient. You could encourage people to talk and pray for each other in twos and threes if that seems appropriate.

BREAD

Fast food – MacDonalds, Burger King, KFC – walk in, order, eat, burp – all over in minutes.

But homemade bread is not made quickly.

Imagine sitting in a warm kitchen, feeling hungry, watching someone making bread.

> *...measuring flour, mixing yeast, sugar and water, making the dough, kneading it...*

The dough is put in a bowl and left to rise – a warm, yeasty smell fills the kitchen. Your hunger grows just thinking about the crusty, fresh bread to come.

But you have to wait...

> *...more kneading and shaping. Placed in the loaf tin, the dough looks closer to fulfilling its potential – but it's left to rise once more...*

And you have to wait...

Into the oven, another wait, more intense smells, growing hunger, a temptation to eat anything – but no, you'll wait for crusty, fresh bread ...

Finally the bread is ready. And you have to wait for it to cool...

Are you hungry for God? Are you waiting for God to answer your prayer, to satisfy your need?

Perhaps like homemade bread, God cannot be rushed. Perhaps like yeast silently breathing and growing, something is happening unseen. Perhaps you need to wait a little longer.

Take some dough and knead it in your hands. Breathe in the warm, yeasty smell. Think about what it could become. Tell God about your hunger – ask God to satisfy your need. Tell God about your unanswered prayers, about what it's like to wait.

David despaired that God would ever answer his prayer and come and help him. He felt abandoned and alone. Read Psalm 13 – and look how it ends.

David affirms his trust in God, in spite of still waiting. He decides to trust and chooses to thank God in spite of feeling so desolate. Can you? Eat some bread as a way of saying that you will trust God to satisfy your hunger and to answer your prayer.

PRAYER ENCOUNTER

A Walk In The Desert

Scripture Focus: Isaiah 35:1-7

Type of Prayer: confession, transformation

Time Needed: 45 minutes

Supplies:

A large plastic sheet, at least 4ft square – you can buy plastic 'dust sheets' from hardware stores for decorating. Get a strong one because damp sand can be quite heavy.

Sand – you can get sand for children's sandpits from toyshops, or use builders sand from a hardware store, although be aware that the yellow color can stain. Use two or three bags of sandpit sand – about 20 kilos.

Slips of paper and pens.

Seven or eight Bibles to place around the sand.

Jugs of iced water – the cooler the better – and glasses, so every participant can take a drink.

Some towels for people to get the sand off their feet. Have one for every five or six participants.

A copy of the handout for each participant. You can download full-size copies of the handouts from www.authenticmedia.co.uk.

OVERVIEW

Life is so busy these days that it is often hard to find time to stop and pray. This prayer encounter gives an opportunity to press pause and look back over the last week. Inspired by the 40 days that Jesus spent in the desert at the start of his ministry, it provides a microcosm of desert peace and a chance for people to reflect on their need for repentance and forgiveness.

Each participant will have a copy of the handout. Guided by this, they will take off their shoes and walk in some sand to think about the impression they have made on others over the last week. They will then walk through the sand again, putting their feet in the same places, and reflect on whether they have followed Jesus or gone their own way. They will write prayers asking for forgiveness and bury these in the sand, leaving them behind. They will think about the areas in their life where they need to experience God's Spirit and will write these with their finger in the sand. They will read from Isaiah 35:1-7 where God promises streams of water and blossoms in the desert. Finally they will drink cool water to symbolize receiving God's forgiveness and they can put sand in their pockets to remind them of this time. Read through the handout to familiarize yourself with what will happen.

SETUP

Spread out the plastic sheet and put the sand on top. Pile up the sand a bit in the middle for people to bury their prayers in. Put the pens, papers and Bibles in two or three places around the edge so people don't have to move too far to get them. Similarly, have a couple of tables where people can get a glass of water – or once you have seen that people have buried their prayers, take them a glass of water.

THE ENCOUNTER

You don't need to do much to lead this encounter other than create an appropriate space and give people copies of the handout. You could introduce the theme at the start and then lead everyone in prayer at the end. Otherwise just leave people to enjoy the space and spend time with God. This needs a sense of space and peace for it to work well. If you have enough leaders and an appropriate building, set this up in the church and run a café or other activities in the church hall. Groups of about six can go and do the worship experience while the others stay in the church hall. At the end, bring everyone together and pray.

Extra

The season of Lent would be appropriate for this time of prayer because it is traditionally a time of fasting and repentance in preparation for Easter. It is a time for self-examination – an opportunity to pause and take stock of our life's direction. However, you can do this exercise at any time of the year.

A WALK IN THE DESERT

How did you get here? Replay your journey in your mind, consciously leaving behind all the things you need to do, the people you need to speak to, the expectations that others have of you.

At the start of his ministry Jesus spent 40 days in the wilderness, alone. At other times he spent nights on a mountain in prayer, talking to his Father.

This is your time – this is your desert. This is your space to be with God, and God is here. Breathe deeply – enjoy the space.

Take off your shoes and socks and walk in the sand. Look at the footprints you have made.

Think back over this last week – what footprints have you left behind you? What impression have you left on the people you have met? Have you trampled on anyone, put anyone down? Do you need to ask forgiveness? Write a prayer to God on a piece of paper.

Walk in the sand again, putting your feet in exactly the same places that you walked before.

Think back over this last week – have you followed Jesus? Have you gone where he has led you, or chosen your own path? Do you need to ask forgiveness? Add this to your prayer.

Now roll the paper up, and as you hold it, ask for God's forgiveness. Leave the paper buried in the center of the sand.

Deserts are dry, dusty places. Think about the areas of your life where you feel dry and in need of God's spirit. Write these in the sand in front of you with your finger – just for you and God to see. When you have finished, smooth the sand again for the people who will come after you.

Read Isaiah 35: 1–7. God promises streams of water in the desert. He promises forgiveness and joy to those who ask for it. Drink some cool water and receive God's forgiveness.

Stay and enjoy God's presence.

When it's time to go, put some sand in your pockets to remind you of meeting God here.

PRAYER ENCOUNTER

Harvest

Scripture Focus:	Matthew 9:35-38; Matthew 13:1-23; Ephesians 6:19-20
Type of Prayer:	intercession
Time Needed:	one hour
Supplies:	Information about mission organizations.
	Cushions.
	Five or six Bibles.
	Small flowerpots, enough for one each.
	A copy of the handout for each participant. You can download full-size copies of the handouts from www.authenticmedia.co.uk.
	The title of each station on a piece of card.
	Sheets of plastic to protect the floor.
	Soil – get a bag of potting compost from a garden center or hardware store.
	Seeds in a bowl – sunflower seeds work well. You need one for each participant plus more for visual effect.
	Small watering can.
	Pile of dried weeds, brambles and branches.
	Pruning shears – two or three pairs.
	Grapes – a small bunch for each person.
	Additional materials to create a stimulating visual display at each station – a garden fork, trowel, gardening gloves – several pairs, stones, small weeds, seed packets, gardening books, large watering can, bottles of liquid plant food, bags for garden rubbish, pots of plants, vegetables just out of the ground.

OVERVIEW

Jesus told several parables about farmers and harvest, which is not surprising because that is what a lot of the people around him were involved in. And the process of planting a seed, tending it, protecting it and waiting for harvest is a brilliant metaphor for what happens when people respond to the word of God and put their faith in Christ.

This prayer encounter provides a time of focused prayer for mission, enabling people to pray for individuals and organizations working in evangelism as well as for friends and family that they are sharing their faith with. Guided by the handout, participants will visit five different stations taking a small flowerpot with them. At the first they will pray for those who prepare the way for God's word to be heard and they will fill their pot with earth. At the second they will pray for those who preach the gospel or share their faith and they will plant a seed in their pot. Next they will pray for those who have begun to open up to God, that the beginning of their faith will be nurtured and developed; here they will water their pot. At the fourth station they will pray for protection for new Christians and they will cut back weeds. Finally they will pray for a time of harvest, for people to put their faith in Christ and they will eat grapes. Because people need to travel round the stations in order, you can provide an area where they can read Bible passages and about mission organizations to inform their prayers as they wait to start.

SETUP

You will need quite a large room to set up the five stations as well as having an area where people can read about mission organizations as they wait to go round. The stations can be as simple or as elaborate as you like. Try to create a good visual display at each one that will help people develop the metaphor of gardening to inform their prayers. Ask some keen gardeners to help you.

Starting place – Put some cushions on the floor in a ring with the mission information in the middle. Have a few Bibles open at the following passages, or print the passages out on sheets of paper: Matthew 9:35-38; Ephesians 6:19-20; Matthew 13:1-23. Put the flowerpots and handouts here for people to collect before they go round. Write or print the title of each station on a piece of card so people can read their handout to see what to do – the titles are in bold on the sample handout.

Preparing the ground – Spread the potting compost out on a sheet of plastic. Add other gardening tools such as a garden fork, trowel and gardening gloves, and some small stones or weeds around the edge, as if they have been pulled out of the soil.

Planting – Put some seeds in a bowl. Add some different seed packets and some gardening books as if someone was planning what they are going to plant.

Watering and feeding – Cover the floor with a plastic sheet to protect it if necessary. Fill a small watering can with water that people can use to water their plants. Have a larger watering can and some bottles of liquid plant food to add to the display.

Weeding and protection – Cover the floor with a plastic sheet to protect it if necessary. Pile up some old weeds, brambles and branches. Put the secateurs on the floor in front. Add the type of bags that you would use for garden rubbish and some more gardening gloves.

Harvest – Put some small bunches of grapes in a bowl. If it's the right season, add some fruit or vegetables that have just been taken from the ground, or some pots of beautiful flowers – anything that shows the end result of gardening!

THE ENCOUNTER

This needs very little in the way of leading. Gather everyone together at the start to introduce the theme, give everyone a copy of the handout and commit the time to the Lord in prayer. Tell people about any particular mission organizations that your church supports, or evangelistic initiatives in the area if that is appropriate. People will move round the different stations at their own pace and will finish the prayer encounter at different times, so invite them back to the start to read some more, or have another room or a space where they can go and drink coffee together and talk. After about an hour, lead a prayer in this room to end the prayer encounter.

38

Extra

If the weather is good, it would be brilliant to set up this prayer encounter in a garden or even on a farm. Participants could actually do some gardening as they pray – digging soil at the first station, watering the garden as well as their pot at the third, pulling up real weeds at the next station and so on.

Extra

Instead of giving a handout to each person, you could put the appropriate words on cards at each station to tell people what to do.

HARVEST

Jesus said, 'The harvest is plentiful but the workers are few. Ask the Lord of the harvest, therefore, to send out workers into his harvest field.'

Collect a flowerpot and visit the different stations to pray about mission. Pray for friends and family who don't yet know Jesus as well as organizations and individuals who do the work of evangelists.

Preparing the ground – Soil needs to be broken up, free form weeds and stones, and full of nutrients to enable plants to grow. Pray for those who prepare the way for God's word to be heard by building relationships, breaking down barriers and serving people with love. Fill your flowerpot up with soil as you pray.

Planting – Once the soil is ready, a seed needs to be planted if anything is to grow. Pray for those who preach the gospel and those who talk to their friends about Jesus. Pray for those who demonstrate the Kingdom of God through the way they live. Take a seed and plant it in your pot as you pray.

Feeding and watering – A seed needs food and water to grow. Pray for those who have begun to open up to God that the beginning of their faith will be nurtured and developed. Add some water to your pot as you pray.

Weeding and protecting – Often weeds grow alongside plants, threatening to choke and overwhelm them. Pray for new Christians that they won't be distracted by the enemy or the voices of the world. Use the secateurs to cut down some of the weeds as you pray.

Harvest – The harvest is plentiful but the workers are few. Pray for many people to commit their lives to Jesus. Pray for evangelists to be fruitful and blessed in the work they are doing. Eat some grapes as you pray.

Remember that it takes time for plants to grow. Pray for encouragement and persistence for all those engaged in mission as you wait for God's Spirit to work. Take your pot home and continue to pray as you watch your plant grow.

Indexes

In these indexes,
PI stands for the shorter Prayer Ideas;
PE stands for the longer Prayer Encounters

INDEX – BIBLE PASSAGES

TRANSFORMING PRAYER

Genesis 8:22 [PI 5]

Joshua 4:1-9 [PI 4]

1 Samuel 7:2-6 [PI 1]

Psalm 13 [PE 1]

Psalm 88 [PI 5]

Isaiah 35:1-7 [PE 2]

Isaiah 53:4-6 [PI 10]

Isaiah 58:1-9 [PI 6]

Amos 5:24 [PI 3]

Matthew 9:35-38 [PE 3]

Matthew 13:1-23 [PE 3]

Romans 1:8-10 [PI 8]

2 Corinthians 2:14-16 [PI 7]

Ephesians 3:20,21 [PI 6]

Ephesians 6:19-20 [PE 3]

Colossians 2:13-15 [PI 10]

1 Thessalonians 5:16-18 [PI 2]

Rev 22:1-5 [PI 9]

42

INDEX – TYPES OF PRAYER

INDEX – TYPE OF ACTIVITY

INDEX – THEMES